then came the

VOICE

VOLUME III

Wording

 FriesenPress

One Printers Way
Altona, MB R0G 0B0
Canada

www.friesenpress.com

ISBN
978-1-03-911875-1 (Hardcover)
978-1-03-911874-4 (Paperback)
978-1-03-911876-8 (eBook)

1. POETRY, SUBJECTS & THEMES, WOMEN AUTHORS

Distributed to the trade by The Ingram Book Company

Table of Contents

Puis vint cette voix
Environ l'heure de midi,
Au temps de l'été,
Dans le jardin de mon père.

Jeanne D'Arc

to the judges at her trial

And then came the voice
Approximately at noon,

In the summertime,
Inside my father's garden.

Author's Translation

"Behold! It is the eve of time,
the hour when the wanderers
turn toward their resting place.
One god after another is coming home...
Therefore, be present...."

Friedrich Holderlin
1770–1843

Quoted in *The Ever-Present Origin* by Jean Gebser (102)
authorized translation by Noel Barstad with Algis Micku

Secret Earth
Photo by Author

"That living word awakened my soul,
gave it light, hope, joy, set it free!"

Helen Keller, *The Story of My Life*

To Michelle, Simone, Bernie, and Paul Decosse
Love has been the glue.

To my five much loved nephews

To our grandmother, Amma Stefanía Helgason, who also wrote poetry,

and to Grandpa Phoenix Decosse, who loved nature and believed
in tomorrow.

Acknowledgements

To my husband, Stuart Capstick. You carry my work in your heart. You quote my poems, and you hum my songs. Your love encourages and supports me every step of the way. I have yet to figure out how the universe delivered us to each other. Thank you forever. There is no end!

To my friend and study-buddy, Michael Devine, who *knows!* You recognized in the poetry what I was too immersed to see. We've capered together through books and ideas and shared an exhilarating adventure of the mind and of the spirit.

To Simone Decosse, my beloved sister, for your help reviewing my manuscript and proofing my book revision. We are a team.

To my beloved grandchildren, Ian, Paige, and Piper Taylor, who every day are my joy and inspiration. Love, Grandma

To my treasured friends, you know who you are. How did I get so lucky!

To my helpful and friendly publishing facilitators at FriesenPress.

Thank you.

Louise

Preface

The Title

My friend, Marie La Perrière from Québec, introduced me some time ago to Jeanne d'Arc's quatrain. It became the basis of an inspiration for the main title of this body of poetry. Recently, I listened to the French author François Cheng speak about this quatrain. He said that it was "a text which comes from the bottom of the heart, but which is the result of an entire life," pointing out that "it is a perfect quatrain, 5-7-5-7." He added, "There is an accent of the eternal to it, and at the same time, it is simple and sublime. It is one of the most beautiful voices of France... Keep in mind this was before she went to the stake. When fully understood in its context, it is an emotive text."

For the reader's listening pleasure, I recommend a lovely musical rendition of Jeanne's quatrain: Et vint cette voix, la musique de Léonie May 8, 2020, available through the Internet.

The Disposition

Since the 1990s I kept together the poems I had written, never thinking for a moment that they might someday become the basis for a book. Now, years later, I considered making a single volume of them, but that threatened to be a book far too big and cumbersome, and an impossible intensity of poems for anyone to face. I didn't want a tome but small volumes that left space for the poems and the reader to slowly land together, to pause, to breathe, to connect, to allow for the poetic exchanges happening between them.

I have always been a lover of liminal places, understanding that the between place is often the most fertile and creative ground. It is where the real alchemy of life's encounters occurs and works its magic. In the case of the poetry, the poem meets the reader, and the reader meets the poem, and something new happens. What a marvelous exchange! What a new and beautiful perfume they've created! For the poem is nothing without the reader.

I decided upon three volumes, but how would I make the selection... by years, by favourites, by themes? In the end, I preferred the arbitrary division of their alphabetical order, which is really no order at all, and involves no hierarchy of preference. The title for each is easily inter-changeable with that of its companion volumes, and each fits in its own way the general *esprit* of my endeavour. And I would keep the over-arching title I had already chosen for the full collection: *THEN CAME THE VOICE*. These, then, are three sister volumes, and it is my hope they may remain connected.

We are talking about poems ranging over a thirty- to forty-year span, so one might easily expect shifts in perspective and in maturity, perhaps made more noticeable by the fact that poems from earlier years inter-mingle closely with poems written a few decades later. For that reason, I included their date of completion at the bottom of each. A good poem, though, is usually universal in its nature, and it matters not when it was written. One challenge then is to write that which stands the test of time.

PLEASE NOTE: This conversation may be continued by turning to the back of the book, to the AUTHOR'S NOTE.

Au clair de la lune: A curious little French folksong. The writer has hurried to his friend Pierrot's in the moonlight to borrow a pen. "Lend me your pen, my friend. My candle is out, and I haven't a pen. For the love of God, open your door!"

"I don't have a pen! I'm in my bed," answers Pierrot. "Go ask the neighbour!"

Pierrot

Au clair de la lune,
Mon ami Pierrot,
Prête-moi ta plume pour écrire un mot.

I fumbled in the night for a stick and a flare,
anything so I could write the huge words
of the huge mind that had just passed through mine.

Ma chandelle est morte,
Je n'ai plus de feu,
Ouvre-moi ta porte, pour l'amour de Dieu!

For the love of God, Pierrot, open your door!
I've neither light, nor pen, and I must write down these words!
Oh god, I mustn't let them slip away!

Je n'ai pas de plume, je suis dans mon lit.
Va chez la voisine, Pierrot répondit…I feel the edges soften
and the pieces slide away from my mind into oblivion.

But the great thought, it illuminated the night, and me, and the stars!
…How could I forget; it was so beautiful!
Get out of bed, Pierrot, and open the damn door!

But by the time this sleepy-head had come,
I was emptied of that comet mind.
I collected the cinders, weeping, praying it would pass through
me again.

May 2021

Pneuma

Who can split the wind,
The where-within of the wind?
Who can split the wind
And get inside?

February 1993

Pushy Gurus

I am weary of pushy gurus.
Of self-appointed critics and fake visionaries,
of misery prophets, and tedious preachers.

Oh, hollow wisdom and noisome clamour!

Pick me...Mine is the way!
Take this path...hear me...
Learn how to...and...Follow me!
You need only pay this amount!
You can do it by instalment.
Give more! Do more! Be more! Have more!
Buy, buy, buy!

Their hollow placard messages mutilate!

For shame! Detach! Connect! Evolve! Organic! DOOMED!
Face your shadow! Heal your pain!
Find your soul mate! Get rich! Be trendy!
Kill the ego! Know the Rapture!
BE SAVED, BY THIS WEEKEND!

I am weary of the self-appointed chosen,
And those who "know" Jesus, the Prophet, and Truth.
And weary, too, of all the fatal "isms"
That assail and flail, blare and scare.

It is a mile-high circus tent
With high-flying artists in glitzy costumes.
I am the smiling clown down below
With the big tear on her cheek and the clumsy feet.

Starting March 30, you can have
a free prayer sent directly
to your inbox, twice a week!
Be honest like me! And another scandal hits the news.

Be silent! Be very still and listen.
There is a world of people to feed, birthdays to celebrate,
And children to love this awakening day.
There's a garden to tend, a lover to greet, a friend to visit.
And there is the blessed silent night for dreaming.

March 2010

Release

You howl to the red-eyed moon!
The betrayal and the contempt,
The sorrow, the despair, and the resistance.
The red-hot rage that strips flesh from bone!

Until defeat, that final note, stops you dead.
And in the dying, a new understanding:
Anger has always stripped away too much.
Expectation has stripped away more.

Now, the silence, vast and empty.
You gently probe that hollow place,
Remember its teeth and turn away.
Not an ending, but a first step.

The second step comes with prayer:
In the name of love, I release you
From my expectations, my hubris, my ignorance.
Your way is not mine, and that's alright!

I release you, sister, brother, stranger, friend.
I release you too, my love, even unto death, for,
If it is your time, I cannot beg you to stay.
And with compassion, I release myself too.

We are free to be what we might be!
The gift and the grace of it lie within us.

June 2016

Remind me

Remind me
Of the things I once knew,
Remind me.

Of that non-remembered life,
That non-remembered love,
Remind me.

Remind me
Of that blue liquid time
When fishes swam beside me,

When curved time caught my wings
And delivered me across the universe
To your secret temple.

Remind me
Of the freedom and the prayer of it,
And of a sweet music called home.

Remind me.

May 2016

Response

(Inner Companion)

What do I do when joy
Feels too big to contain?

Be a subtle sun
And shine it back to the world.

2013

Reverie at Island View Beach

Of all the experiences that Over-Mind enjoys
In its constant play as matter,
The most exquisite must be as Ocean.

To languorously stretch, as the sea is doing today,
Deliciously shivering
Under the feathery touch of a soft breeze...

To rise, and curl lightly inward, up, and over;
Then splash into a thousand sparkling ripples
That delicately lap the welcoming shore...

To flaunt its blueness under the blue firmament,
Wantonly offering itself
To the ardent heat of a love-mad sun...

To become a looking glass
For these gazing hills and forests, that ask:
"Who is the most beautiful of all?"

"Why, you are, World, you are!"

Ah, were I deity itself,
I would worship myself as the ocean.

September 2009

Sandalwood and Rose

In the cradle of rejoice,
Sandalwood and Rose
Stir awakenings and expansions,
Exchanges and emanations,
Inter-penetrations of soul qualities.

Sandalwood and Rose

Give rise to intuitions and invitations...
Inspirations conveyed with a subtle touch
In the subtle language of essences and energies.

Sandalwood and Rose

Messages composing new pathways
Of waves and frequencies, of attraction and desire.
Fingertip tendrils,
Reach for each other with
Carefully placed soul offerings
That linger and shape themselves
Into the whispered life of joy unsurpassed,
Gently pressed messages into the heart:

　　You are so loved!
　　You are so loved!

...Aftermaths of silent wonder
Shaped into
The after-scent of perfume....

December 2020

Scared Silly

It scared me silly, you know, to stick out my neck.
That's why you never saw these poems before.
It scared me silly to expose myself,
to let you see so much of me, for
writing poetry has been a large part of who I am.

It scared me silly to imagine how you might have
casually tossed aside my offerings and walked away.
With what censorious dismissal you might have treated them.
Or how you might have shredded my psychology.

I cringed to see my soft underbelly exposed and tested
in the waters of a critic's cavilling eye.
For I have been the wild fox of Saint-Exupéry's Le Petit Prince

Don't domesticate or hunt me, he said.
Let us first establish ties, and then I will come to you
because we have established a relationship of trust.
We will tame each other.

It scares us silly to really open to each other, doesn't it?
But to trust each other becomes the gist and the thrust of our raison de faire.
I don't ask you to think as I do, not ever!
But let us consider the possibility of what we might offer each other in time:

Can we...
Would we...
Indifferently toss each other aside?
...And what about our uncertainties?

In this, I can only speak for myself.
I trust these poems; I love them, and I stand by them.
I have striven for. and won, faithfulness to myself.
It endows me with a gentle protective power to offer them to you.

> *For this is my tenderly planted garden,*
> *Each flower lovingly placed for eternity.*

October 2020

Seasoned

I am well-seasoned.

"Thyme" has measured my footsteps
And "sagely" seduced me to try
The meandering paths of experience.
"Mary" as a rose in spring,
I have chased the unchasable,
Dreamed the impossible,
Challenged the un-do-able.
The salt of experience is mine

And I am well-peppered too
With the heat of my trials.
No stranger to "saffron" am I.
Why, I have "mustard" my courage
When wine-splashed nights made mock of day!
Yea, and "chili" winds but stiffened my spine!
I have enriched my mind with the butter of books
And thickened my blood with the hearty broth of sea and sky.
Love was the deepest flavour of all.

I am well-seasoned.

In this mellow time of autumn,
The honeyed fruit of memory moves deep in my veins.
Life risked, life lived, life shared.
Sorrow and love,
Failure and success,
And questions, always questions.

Stir, stir, stir.
Simmer, simmer, simmer.
Is this dish ready?
Taste me, my love, taste me.

January 2003

Seventy

Today is my seventieth birthday
And I celebrate its rich significance.
It is the great count of moments,
That grand unity of minutes and seconds
That birthed my extraordinary life.

Seventy. Will no one acknowledge it?
Instead, your denials and fears impose themselves:
"Don't worry, it's just a number."
"It doesn't mean anything."
"You're only one day older than yesterday."
"Bah! You're as young as you feel!"
Your words dismiss the honesty of it!

Seventy is a rite of passage.
The years flow broadly through my veins, a rich fluid
That carries the meaning of everything my life has been:
Every shift and quiver, every sensibility that informed me.
Today is my past and my youth, pressing into tomorrow
Through the narrow connective passage of this one day.
It is a gathering of self, a threshold, a new departure.

Seventy carries a beauty and a maturity of soul
That deserve to be profoundly engaged with.
I am no longer a new snowflake on a mountain top,
I am the river moving closer, ever closer to the sea.
That too is a grand celebration when one understands.
I am seventy.
I love the grace of it, and I joyously embrace
The astounding voyage that lies ahead.

April 16, 2017

Shadowed Hills

Night creeps up the canyon walls.
It shapes the shadowed hills and cliffs
And rises to meet itself in a twilit sky.

I follow
Drawn past the anytime
Of Earth-time
And past countless cosmic eons
Of stellar events, both new and long ago spent.

That great unknown is as vast and beautiful
As surrender
And as familiar as the space within my heart
Where countless suns and moons
Of living galaxies beckon
And are born.

The body is but a membrane
A mere contemplation
Straddling two aspects
Of the one great coming forth.
Gazing outward, I fall into that
Which is happening within.

Vibrant, birthing Universe,
Am I expanding into you,
Or are you unfolding
Deep inside me?

February 2010

Shapeshifter

I once found it very hard
To stand confidently in my own truth.

The problem was wanting the impossible.
You couldn't change for me, although I wanted you to.

The tragedy lay in me that I was young
And could not yet hold high my own candle.

I became a shapeshifter to survive.
The success today is that I am an elder,
Content to have no shape at all.

January 2017

Sinai Dreaming

A hawk wheels with slow, sweeping grace
In the blue space of sky-without-end.
High on a granite ledge, whitened
By an intense Sinai sun, I gaze at the hawk,
And with dreaming eyes, lazily trace
Its lofty unhurried trajectory.
The world shimmers like a mirage
And soul seeps out; gently ascends,
Seeks, then merges with the hawk.
For a timeless moment I am
A creature of the high blue winds.

...being is a dreaming in slow lazy circles
above a golden, light-filled valley
...being is a dreaming stillness of wing
carried on cooling currents of air
above the hot breath of a desert in trance
...being is the perfection of air-born tranquility,
freedom from the gravity and gravitas
of earth-bound lives.

Utter peace.

March 2017

Sing

O Humanity Divine,
This is our glorious day!
In the clear and perfect light of breaking dawn,
let us walk together the holy road of Mecca
and pray to her most compassionate
Mother Guan Yin.
Come!
Step inside the Medicine Wheel,
smudge each other with sweet grass,
then lift the sacramental cup of Ayahuasca.
Let us visit as one family the graves of our ancestors
and sit in meditation before the Buddha.
Come!
Celebrate Shabbat, dance merrily with the Lord Krishna.
The time has come
to step lightly upon this sacred ground of our beloved Earth.

The time has come
to sit at the feet of the world; raise joy-filled voices to the cosmos.
The time has come to be
a fellowship of creatures, a harmony of humanity,
a community of good and sharing people.
Shanti, Salaam, Shalom, Peace!
Gracias, Arigato, Hiy, Hiy!
Amen.

March 2018

Snowless November

November woods.
Earth tones singing in muted keys
Of brown and grey minor...
Feathery hues of a horned owl
A prairie chicken
A black-capped chickadee.

Chicka-dee-dee-dee!

Tiny sounds are so quiet in silence
...a woodpecker
Mouse-rustles in dry grass
And the silent high-pitched hum
Of red cranberries,
Discrete berry ornamentals
Like muted piccolos.

And there, and there, and there,
Single droplets of leaf,
Suspended precariously
From naked limbs on naked trees.
A final golden note
...Sustained...
And then farewell.

The goose is gone; the deer waits
Hidden behind dusty brush and poplar,
And amidst the reek of musk,
Rusty leaf rot, and sweet grasses.
Earth-ness
In the layered strains
Of half-remembered autumns.

And like a musician-artist,
Downy air has softly erased all that stands
Linear and separate

And smudged into seamless connection
All the things of earth and sky
And in-between.

November 2013

Soldier Child

When they sent you blithely off to fight
carrying a gun,
convinced of your own heroism,
you couldn't understand
that the price you would pay
would redeem no one,
least of all yourself.

March 2017

Somebody Combed the Clouds

Somebody combed the clouds today.
They lie wavy, thin, and white

Upon the silken sky,
Like an old woman's hair
Fanned across her blue pillow.

Sometimes I wonder at a conceit that frames
All things of nature in human terms.

And I wonder too how it would be
To know the other in terms of itself
...sky as sky, eagle as eagle, tree as tree.

The honesty of it all might kill us,
Unless it didn't.
And then we might learn new things

...What it is to breathe under water
To glide on air
To graze in the meadow with the deer.

The honesty of it all might save us.

2016

S o u l

With a sustained sigh,   lips pressed gently to his ear,

hands pressed lightly to his chest,

Soul croons her love for him

garlands of ethereal song delicately encircling his body,

breathy,

lingering invocations of love.

Melodious tones, like streams of moonlight,

penetrating his skin,

suffusing his core,   so that,

at long last,
he stands in soft surrender.

She comes   inviting more than just his attention,

recognizing neither formal doorways, nor parsed time,
neither conventional spellings, nor fabricated heavens.

She comes by natural pathways,   where distance is nonexistent,

language has no words,

and undersongs guide poets and other star gazers of the heart.

She emerges   out of her cosmic interiority,

out of love and necessity,

inviting more than just your attention,

urging more than just my mind.

April 2019

Spring

Modest spring is stepping out
With Robin, Magpie, and me.
Attending promises of green
sway in the caress of warm air.
Sunlight ripples through the spruce trees;
Seagulls wheel in broad blue circles,
Where even the perfect clouds are too lazy to drift.
"Here I am!" calls Chickadee.
"**What**?" squawks Magpie.
This is a rare peace that shouldn't be missed.

May 2018

Stripped!

We come into the world naked
And we leave it denuded,
Stripped,
Not with an expectation
But with a hope and a prayer.
With a trust that the beauty we had so loved
And beheld in the arms of the world
Was but a remnant that had fallen
From the benevolent hands of a maker
Who, in her own compassion,
Had kindly let escape
Some promise of an origin to which,
Leaving all,
It was foreseen
That we would return in the end.

October 2020

Sunday

I woke up and it was Sunday.
What a nice sunny morning it was too!
And on this sunny Sunday morning,
Stumbling through the fog cloud of my mind,
I felt all the Sunday things
That a lifetime of Sundays inspires.

It isn't so much the things you do,
But the Sunday feeling you don't ever lose.
You recognize it with every breath of your day:
A quietness and an absence of ordinary business,
When time expands, and you forget your troubles.
Contemplating the freedom to be lazy, to drift,
To read, to hang out, to chat, to enjoy, to be bored.
A book, a beach, a friend, a snooze, the Sunday roast...
And trying not to think of that dreaded Monday.

It's strange, but on Sundays
No adventure awaits, but the ritual
Of filling a stopped-ness of everything the week had been.
It's the atmosphere ...
A dreaming, suspended time
That began long ago in childhood, and
Has shaped the happy lassitude of Sundays ever since.

I woke up and it was Sunday.
And with that Sunday feeling
Moving deep in my blood,
I washed and dressed and thought about the day.
What might we do, and who might I call?

I woke up on a nice sunny Sunday,
And toppled off a time cliff into Wednesday afternoon.
Three lost days! What happened to time?
It really shocks a body, you know.

July 2020

Sunset Robe

We circumscribe ourselves
With our biases, our arrogance, and our fears.
We shut out the exquisite,
The diaphanous,
And are left holding the grosser aspects
Of experience, of life, and of ourselves.
We flounder and we sink
Under the weight of the unbeautiful
Because there is no light.
Because there is no clarity.

There was a teacher
Whose robe was the colour of sunset.
He blessed me once
With eyes that saw forever,
And then sent me on my way
Not with a word,
But with a look,
A blessing
Now grown like a garland,
Infusing the rest of my life
With the fragrance of possibility.

The years passed,
The teacher too departed.
A breath of jasmine lingers.
A breath of sweetness endures,
Has transformed parts of this earth
Into realities that float
Upon a finer and softer air,
A subtle goodness
Interpenetrating all.

In a time of need,
An act of kindness
Puts into my hands
His robe the colour of sunset.
But it is not a robe, you see!
It is presence, exquisite and diaphanous,
From the eyes of the one who saw forever,
Reminding me of garlands and of jasmine.

September 2020

The Essential Self

*A dream teaching about
Amazonian mother plant, Ayahuasca.*

*"The Mother breaks down blockages
and false beliefs,
but she does not break down
the basic structure that is you.
And you should not ask for that.
The constructs of ego are not you.
The blockages are not you.
These parts can get flushed away.
But the structure that is you
must stand, always.
It is that which is your basic stability of being.
It is the essential self."*

February 2018

The Eyes of Blue and the Eyes of War

The Eyes of Blue and the Eyes of War
See the littered ground of life
And struggle to gain Utopia.

You won't get peace with a rally,
nor wrest it from the lords of battle.
And whose truth will it be?

But when doing turns to being
In the middle of the heart space,
Then Love loves you into your greater humanity.

Tundra eyes see further.
In the white distance of snow,
They see the wholeness of it all and surrender.

Anything else is just another slow dying
on the lonely plane
of separations.

November 2010

The Flower and the Honeybee

I drift in the drowsy heat of a summer's day.
My book slips away, and with softened focus,
My dreaming eyes wander into the trees, the grass, the sky...
Wander...and come to rest on the big blue pot
Where a riotous mass of yellow blossoms
Shout and tumble in every direction.
I drop into their yellow brilliance,
Surrender to their exuberance.

A honeybee buzzes into our midst, causing a great stir.
Now follows a tremulous becalming
As each blossom anticipates her own glorious encounter.
The bee, with deep concentration, embraces each flower,
Buries himself sensuously into her honeyed center.
No flower receives less attention; no flower is less worthy.
Pretty, faded, broken, young or old, the bee sees nothing of that,
Cares only for the flower's succulent offerings.

One flower draws me by the intensity of her suspense.
I fall into her deep sigh.
I feel the quiver that travels up her slender stem
And lodges like a small shock inside her golden centre.
I feel her open wide, impatiently wanting!
...until, with a deeper sigh, she rapturously surrenders.

A sublime moment of participation
In the passionate sacrament of life.

August 2018

The Gift of your Gaze

Sometimes,
I am so fortunate
As to lift my eyes
And catch the private moment
When you look at me.
Your heart is in your eyes,
And I am made so very tender
By the gentle purity of your love.
In these glowing, naked moments of grace,
I quietly accept
The gift of your gaze
And thank
The generous confluence of tides
That made possible our joining.

January 2018

The Heart Sings Sideways

Love doesn't live in ivory towers,
It doesn't live on flagpoles or banners either.
The heart sings sideways.
It follows the ley lines of underground sources
To the personal,
To the moment,
To the intimate,
And it falls in love!

   With the pesky ant
   The cheeky chipmunk
   The stumbling old man
   The snotty child
   The handful of soil
   The planet...

It falls in love, and it falls in love, and it falls in love...

October 2018

The Words to Say...

Weep dear friend, weep to empty your heart
of the grievous agony, that has scoured you raw,
but do not carry that ancient wound too long.

I would not wish to enshrine *such pain*.
I would wish woven into a greater field,

part of the rich and continuous stream of life.
Then, benevolence stirs the heart
...a loving acceptance of the whole of life lived
...a gentling power *to feel deeply yet carry lightly*.

It frees one to tap into the genius of the universe.
It inspires a freedom and a joy of learning to play with the gods
in this vast adventure of the heart and the mind.

Not for me the pride of possession.
Pain begs compassion.

It demands forbearance.
It brings us to our knees.
But I remind myself often that it is only *one*
of the many conditions of being alive.
It offers no badge of honour in itself,
nor is it a personal virtue to colonize and defend.
It exists, and none are spared its lashings.
But none need wear it like a crown.

October 2010

There Comes a Time

There comes a time when you know it's hopeless.

Only so many times can you consent to trust again
Only so many times can you endure trust broken
Only so many times can you repair a torn-up heart
Only so many times can you howl to the red-eyed moon.

There comes a time when at last you understand defeat.

And you accept that hope is another expectation
And you wonder how your love survives, but it does
And you wonder how you survive, but you do
And you sing softly to yourself and to the white-faced moon.

June 2016

Time Simultaneous

At times,
Turning into a here,
I bump into a then.
...Fall into a time-layered experience of place
And feel again the sharp taste
Of its first freshness.

A clear vertical time-tunnel opens,
A multi-layered translucence
Of superimposed events...
And like a special-effects camera,
Some faculty penetrates all, sees all at once.

There is access to events of my life
That unfolded throughout the years,
And on this particular corner of place,
And to the immediacy
That gave each moment its authenticity.

There is access too,
To earth histories,
Vibrant, urgent, and pressingly real.
...And futures erupt,
That as yet have no confirmation.

But what of those unfoldings
To which no time can be ascribed,
Where unfathomable images reveal
Beyondnesses and elsewhens
That no historical memory offers?

And about all this, I am compelled to ask:
What is the nature of

    Time and Life,

    Mind and Memory,

    Dream and Imagination,

That makes all this even possible!

August 2018

Toward a Centre of Contemplation

NOTHING:

No thing...Thing
Thing...No thing

What is here, and there, and in between
That makes the difference between a thing and a no thing?
What makes a no thing a thing?
And what erases a thing, and leaves a no thing?

What is there in that
Liminal
In-between
Alchemical space...

That has the power to
Create-destroy
Add-subtract
Transform-erase
Enhance-diminish?

Is it...raw will?

Raw will is a forceful power, a godlike power,
And I ask myself:
To what extent do I embrace it?
And what gloves can I wear that are strong enough
To hold it ...wield it heart-fully and skillfully?
How does one hone raw will to light darkness
Without destroying darkness's inner inherent light?

Is it...raw love?

I know I have scorched other tenderer shoots
With the raw force of exuberant love.
Erasure of a sort?
Yet I have raised a dying spirit with
Tenderly wielded love power;
Coaxed an almost nothing into a nascent something.

Is it...raw hatred?

I have recoiled from this force in fear,
Born of an ethic that eschews all commerce with dark power
But is there yet some *thing* in this,
That serves the alchemical surges of Life's purpose?
And what of all other raw urges that drive or inspire?

No thing... Thing
Thing...No thing

The fear of change...the fear of consequence
The embracing of change...the embracing of consequence
And in-between a force that...places?...erases?

I sense no natural reply.
No organic answer to my
- quandary
- question
- quest

But
From quandary comes gestation,
From question comes generation,
From quest comes genesis.

And the play goes on

The play between opposites
The play of the players
The play of the storyline
The play of the gods
The play of life in all its warts and glory
The play of the five senses, and of the heart, which is the sixth.

Is the heart the filterer of raw power?
Is the heart the liminal knower that
Recognizes and animates
Favours and balances
Shapes and harmonizes with its own intelligence?

Thing...No thing
No thing...Thing
And in between a power of the heart.

Filterings not born of Ethic
But of the wisdom of green shoots, the green shoots of life
That know the formulae of their own existence
And the inspirations of their will to be.

Being: a creative act that never stops.
That only happens when *in-between*
Listens to the wisdom of green shoots.
Life knows itself.

November 2014

Transcendence

The leaves are falling...
gentle lingerings and poignant partings.
But the great elm tree is glorious,
expanded and luminous!
Golden against the blue-sky infinity.

Does the tree let go of the leaf?
Or does the leaf, ripened and seasoned,
let go of the tree?

Farewell, sighs the tree to the leaf,
We'll meet again in summer.
Be not sad, whispers a consoling voice,
it is merely life's way of strengthening and resetting its course again.

Joyous certainty inspires me like the glow of sunlight.
I see the wind and the ever-diminishing sailing leaf.
I see whisps of you, and whisps of me, and all that ever grew,
sailing into blue eternity; I feel a glorious certainty of being:

- Certainty about the soul
- Certainty about the spirit that soars
- Certainty about continuous life...

and about the metaphor that transcends all limitations
and delivers a golden leaf
to the green summer land, ever-present,
hidden
inside endings.

October 2021

Trans-Human Future

When did we sell ourselves to the puppet masters?
Out of what despair did we become a jingle-jangle
Of disconnected sound bites
Clinkety-clanking through scripted, show-time lives?

Behold that New Human:
An iota in a dismembering humanity,
A rootless, disinherited microchip...
Itemized spirit, tipping into the void.

Behold that New Idea:
An endangering-endangered singularity,
Lonely wanderer of a parched Eden,
Trivial and irrelevant in its new landscape.

The green wick is turning brown.
The shrunken fruit falls from a dying tree.
The shriveled leaf clings to the desiccated limb.

Do not think to rescue Nature; the dying is in us
Who have not loved ourselves deeply enough.
Humankind: the last outcast of her own countless betrayals.

Call forth the power of our inner poet
In whose verdant breath
We might re-awaken the green language.
Universes depend upon it.

There is still time to re-member who we are
...life while we know the feel of our own flesh
...hope while there is a heart that beats
...heaven while we can still dream.

There is a deeper imagination to embrace!
A cosmic person struggles to emerge,
Slowly and tenderly self creates!
We may in time give birth to our own magnificence.

September 2015

Transmission

The Mother Plant was coming tonight,
and so, I asked the important question:
Abuelita, I have reached the last quarter of my life.
How do I walk through this garden
with grace and dignity
fulfilling on this earth what I came to do?

In the soft velvet expanse of that Ayahuasca night,
She spoke.
All conversations take place in the heart.
There is no age; there is no death.
There is only life.
Trust; walk forward.
You can always see the light.

And so it was spoken, and so it is.

August 2019

Tristis Paradoxum

There is an engaging map of the world
The gazing upon which offers entrance
Into a contemplative place of renewal.

Evocative blues, greens, and pale gold
Cleanse the mind,
Bathe it in reminders of a planet's wild beauty.

Nearness and distance suspend one loosely over
Oceans and land masses
That spread outward with ease and wild freedom.

Nary a border, a name, or a straight line
Corrupts its dreaming presence,
Its peace of wholeness.

I sink into its utopian paper memory.
Drift for a while in the dream of a human integrity
Still in touch with the root forces of a living planet,
Lest I forget too much in these fractured times.

February 2017

Unencompassed

When my heart trembles with love for you
And you turn away in scorn,
Or render me invisible with your indifference,
I am not crushed.

When I share my passionate musings with you
And you challenge them with cold logic,
Though my arguments melt into puddles
Seared by the heat of your disdain,
I am not silenced.

When my voice is too loud or my acts too irreverent
In that holy place of serious people;
When my joy runs riot in that temple to misery
And condemnation drips from silent stares and stern lips,
I am not extinguished.

When my fingers gently probe the secret folds of life
And draw from its clear heart, like a bow across a string,
An exquisite note that hollows the soul,
Though your shouts of *thou-shalt-not!* deafen me,
I am not shamed.

When I am silent before your gods and offer none of my own,
When I step away from your rituals and impose none of my own,
When I turn from your beliefs and incantations
And am vacant before your flags and your credos,
I am not disinherited.

When I walk through doorways of suffering
And enter rooms of sickness, anger and despair;
When age distorts a youthful countenance
And death looks me coldly in the eye,
I am not undone.

When fear comes thundering down the hall of my five senses
And I am made blind and deaf unto myself;
When panic grows tentacles of insanity that choke all reason
And obscure the clear light of mind,
I am not consumed.

When my actions become distillations of a heart turned away from itself,
And my indifference desecrates the earth and its creatures;
When my acts grow more depraved because I can't bear the stench of my
own deeds;
When my reflection stares back at me in horror and I recoil from my
own monstrosity,
I am not forsaken.

Soul's truth is simple and beautiful:
To step beyond the broken heart
Is to see light shining in the heart of darkness...
And innocence, too, beyond that.

We are born for extravagance:
To stretch and grow; to learn and rejoice; to dance!
Life is an invitation to live, and its power is celebration!

There is no commerce except to share, no place except the centre.
There is no posture but that which embraces,
No time except that which intersects the present act of being.

There can be no judgement in the appreciation of beauty;
No failure except for the things we have carelessly left undone,
And evil is the result of an ignorance, and of things not yet understood.

When the inner compass loses its north
And a world becomes lost in its own darkness,
The only light left is the light each of us is willing to shine
In order to light the way.

2013

Venus Then and Now

I'm a skinny-assed woman, a *domesticated* woman,
and I don't have your big, beautiful, Venus ass
that once swayed
with the slow and stately rhythm
of the long savanna grasses,
...with the pulsing, musky music
of a hot and humid jungle where everything
THRIVED! ALIVE!
And green was so GAUDY
your skin wore its emerald sheen.
You were nature's Queen,
while I forgot you, my own Earth Mama.

I became the ice Queen who didn't warm up.
Your blood was rich and red and true
Mine, a domesticated blue,
thin and cold like Arctic night.
My wounded womb got tame and tight
And I learned I'd always have to fight
just to touch the sacred earth and sacred ground
of our deep and holy feminine body sound.
I don't think my roots go deep enough even now!

Mother Mary was a virgin.
Her sky-body was off limits
her earth-body a painted statue, **bound**
...to the sanctity of power
curdled milk of male power.
Fracturing, fragmenting, raping, desecrating,
it controlled the likes of her and the likes of me.

It washed away our ocean fluids
with stagnant holy water
and with potent punishing arrogance
it damned and dried us up so good
we lost our honeyed womanhood.
We lost those hot, and salty wetnesses,
those sacred, fertile wetnesses...
lush tributaries for nourishing body, mind, and soul.

We got so clean and flat and dry.
that we turned into white paper
and they wrote on us,
yes, they **wrote** on us...big and bold like thunder
Thou shalt not! and **Thou shalt!**

I don't say I haven't been happy
I don't say I haven't been a lover
I don't say my life hasn't been bold or even free.
I fought **hard** to liberate the memory of me.

But one thing I didn't know **enough** to be
was a cherisher of body
...beautiful, sweet girl-body
...rich, fulsome woman-body
...deep, planetary earth-body
...wisdom-bearing soul-body
Poor, crying, dying, abandoned, disappearing body!

I want to take it back.
Yes, and I want to take **You** back!
And our Beautiful!...Swaying!...Luscious!...Big-ass life, too!

...Body of earth, body of ocean
...Body of passion, body of blood
...Body of beauty, body of pain
...Body of song, body of celebration
Oh yes, I call you back, I claim myself in **you**.

I stand and drink your sweet-water rain
that washes away the stain
of that ink
that terrible black ink
that cancelled the body and soul
and my own Beautiful!...Swaying!...Luscious...Big-ass life!

After eons of earth-time, I begin to understand
yes, I *begin* to understand just how beautiful you are.

Mother of Wild, Mother of Earth,
Mother of Body, Mother of Soul,
Mother of Suffering, Mother of Passages,
Mother of Life and Death and Beyond,
I begin to understand just how
mysteriously, terrifyingly, beautiful you are.

And I, your long-lost, *domesticated,* daughter
have *dared!...and dare to ask again*
the deeper questions:

How do I *wear* you?
How do we *move* in each other?
How do **I** open wide and giving, like a rich, red rose
so that **all life** might move
more generously and gloriously in *us*,
O ancient Venus,
O Mother then and now.

July 2016

Warbler Bird

Warbler bird
flashings of olive and gold
among leafy treetops,
singing, warbling, flitting,
cheerfully and splendidly alive.

Swoops, lifts, swoops,
catches shimmering trails
of warm sunlit air,
innocent and ignorant
of silent destiny...

THUMP!

The tiny body breaks
against reflected sky,
against deceiving glass
that tricks and takes
something personal.

Glorious creature,
in the stroke of a moment,
felled!
A tiny poignant stillness,
a tiny feathered finality.

And death
is gone-ness that shocks us
into blankness
- stark and silent.

July 2019

Washing-Away Rain

Wash away, gentle rain,
The soft liquid sadnesses
for which no promise or bargain
can stay your tender course.
The ending and the beginning,
and all our tomorrows, vanished!

Beauty doesn't vanish,
and neither does this:
it is life's promise
to take us through every loss,
and every gain a body can ever know, until
at last, it takes us beyond our last breath.

Wash it all away, gentle rain,
but shower on us your blessings.
I can see through the rain-splashed glass
lingering shades of colour that were our yester-years.

I can see through the rain-splashed glass
lingering smears of mist
that would have been
our nebulous dreams for tomorrow.

Weep for endings, endings unknown and unforeseen,
and losses much harder than ours right now to bear!
For we have loved! And we have dreamed!
And ugliness never sat long at our door
without goodness coming to sit beside us too.

Weep for our love, and for our loved ones,
who themselves must leave one day too;
who must weep and bid goodbye
to their own gentle washed-away lives.

The artist cleans her blurred slate.
New images emerge,
informed by more clearly viewed yesterdays
and more generously lived todays.

The artist clears her smeared slate.
Sees different dreams,
deeper understandings about life,
greater lovings, and freer imaginations.

Weep, gentle washing-away rain,
at the pathos and the beauty of it all.

Despite our many delusions,
we have neither been earth- nor body-bound.

Where we go,
may soft memories accompany us...

Where we go,
may peaceful sensations guide us...

To your sweet-water songs amidst the apple trees,
to their perfumed wetnesses of pink apple breath,
and to the one mind that we become
in the loving arms that carry us.

Sept. 2020

What Is Your Philosophy of Life?

Yours is a hard question to answer but let me try.

I could speak of much respected teachers,
Or of the books I have breathed...but no,
Something primal speaks of another knowing,
And that the book of being is itself all-knowing!

Come!
I will paint for you my dreamings
Whisper you my poems
Sing you my songs
Offer you my gazing eyes.

Come!
Let me collect dewdrops for you from the honeysuckle.
Let me show you wild bees making love with the thistle flower.
Follow me onto ancient goddess ground
Where we will meet her in sacred time.

Come!
Let us ululate with the desert women of rich feminine presence.
Let us celebrate with them the joyful heat that arises from deep living.
Drink richly with me of the wine of living streams
And let us lick together the salt of our sweat and of our tears.

But I cannot invite you into the secret chamber,
Sacred garden of the heart,
Wherein my beloved comes in moon-silvered visions.
The way is my own and solitary.

Not a philosophy, but an engagement...

    joy in movement
    fluidity of rivers
    life embracing itself in living.

Passion on its ecstatic journey home
Though it take a thousand years.
Like the bird that senses its direction,
Like the arrow that seeks its centre,

I breathe, attentive to the inner stirrings of things,
That I might hear the rich and beautiful music of meanings
Wherein the light of Origin shines and awaits
The arrival of its prodigal sons and daughters.

May 2008

What You Forget

When you don't look up into the night sky very often

Because the city lights hide it,
Because the mosquitoes are aggressive,
Or daylight is too long, and you are in bed,

You forget

The compelling enormity of space and distance,
The sensation of being drawn
Into majesty and cosmic presence.

You forget

The exquisite dance of light and dark
Of star-filled firmaments
That play your heart like a harp.

You forget

The red planet and the names of constellations.
Chasing falling stars
And the black immensity of silence.

You forget

How big and how small you are,
And how profoundly right it feels
To release yourself into the mystery.

You forget

...until one sleepless night in August
You step outside, barefoot and naked.
The cottage door slaps shut behind you

But you do not hear it.

August 2012

What's in a word?

Why,
Happiness, my love,

And
The destiny
Of life!

What's in a word?

Why,
the destiny
Of universes, my love!

August 2016

When I Parted the Green Foliage

And when at last
I parted the green foliage of self,
You were there.

You held me close and you cried.
You told me of your great longing
That I should find you.

For eons you called to me.
For eons you stood behind the veil
And begged me to see you.

And all the while you loved me
From behind the diaphanous folds
Of time and space.

February 2012

When You Cried Justice

When you first cried Justice,
I believed you.

But why are you clutching
that pound of flesh so tightly now?
And I
see no justice
in the devastation you've wrought.

September 2021

Where Are You, Kelly Pepper

Where are you, Kelly Pepper?
Perfect child, innocent child,
You visited me today as I sat in quiet contemplation.
Thirty years dissolved and vanished!

Kelly Pepper,

round little face, freckle-dusted
soft brown eyes, long-lashed
chin-length hair, straight cut
bangs like feathers.

Little girl, quiet gentle mouse,
Stillness had been your protection
From a violence too soon revealed by others.

In perfect knowledge
You turned to me, your teacher.
Your face, like the full moon,
Shone with pure trust.

And in your pure trust, for an instant,
I became that perfect being.
You put your hand in mine,
To hold and keep you safe.

Sweet girl, child of Life, thank you.

In your pure trust, I found my own.
We are connected, Kelly Pepper,
In that somewhere out of time,
In that place of life's pure offerings.

2007

Why I Write

I don't write
Because I want to.
It's not an ambition.
I write because I must!
Things write themselves into my heart
Then press urgently upon my pen.
Writing reveals to me
what must be seen.
And so I write
Because I must!
I could
Not,
Not write!

June 2016

Wild Aphrodite

And when I rose from the sea trailing seaweed and cockle shells,
A star came down and lit my brow
For I had been to the centre of everything
Where shadows reveal themselves as rainbows
And angels are musical notes lifting on wings of love
To embrace a love-mad sun that burns with the heat of its
exquisite passion.

And as I stood in the tide pools that cooled my wild and happy heart,
Those sweet and briny tide pools of beginnings,
I breathed myself into the green life of plants that I might rise again
To catch the raindrops falling on my parched earth tongue
That yearned so amorously for their honeyed kisses.

And blue was the colour of freedom,
As I rose to meet a sky that held its sapphire child in its palm,
Like a mother holding her child's heart in her own,
Trailing stars and seaweed and cockle shells...

July 2018

Windflowers

light as air

do not press themselves

upon

the meadow grasses

January 2021

With Angel Voices Heard All Around

1. Wherever separation happens, there is form.

2. Steer for the true north!
said the angel of tomorrow.

3. There is a way, a path exists!
Reach for the high pole of your being.

4. Love is the heart continuum,
the very centre of our incarnations

5. Without the heart,
it is only a house of senses and appetites.

6. Beware of swamps!
The prophet steered his boat on water
and not on land. That is what
saved him and his sail.

7. Tomorrow is not made of yesterday, but of today.
Now is the time to mend it.
It is the secret history of everything!

8. I too live in the dark places.
Love in the dark places.
You must love in the dark places too!

9. Drink from the cup of cleanliness.

10. Moisten and loosen the surrounding soil
to extract the tap root in its entirety.
No other way will remove it all.
Tap roots are the rooted habits
of thought and behavior,
born of spiritual ignorance.

11. The ephemeral life: this now
so elusive, so delicately transparent
when you can see through it.
This place: a bridge between here
and what isn't here.
"Here" is but a shimmer and a dusting.

12. Said the angel of good tidings:
The war is over.
Now forgive and live,
Live and forgive.

The 1960's

Wording

Let my words be trees of green,
Giants of life and exchanges of breath.
Let my words be violets in hidden places,
A language in mauve and of delicate perfections
Nestling among stones and mosses.
Let my words be fields of crocuses,
Harbingers of spring and exuberant rebirth.
Let my words be the fruit of vines and ripened grains
That nourish and delight body and soul.
Let my words be poems, songs, prayers,
Expanding beauty into your heart and mine,
Connecting us to earth and sky.
Let all our words be angels of light
Lifting us and bringing us face to face with each other,
The human and the creaturely,
In a passionate compassion of being.
Let no rock, no bird, no leaf nor drop of water go un-worded,
For there is a word to animate and to reveal
The radiance of everything.
Let our words be inspirations that orient us to
Revelations of deep and truthful theophanies
Which is both our longing and our way home.

April 2018

Words

The philosopher plumbs the depth of words
To better speak her ideas and cogitations.

The poet hears the emerging words that reveal
What has aroused her ardent absorption.

The depth traveler knows there is a limit to words,
And that silence and right-being are oft' the best ambassadors.

June 2016

World Mind

I have donned my earthly gown
To stray in self-created dream.
Out of my completeness
I am become a garden,
Sweet-scented and rich for the senses
Where creatures freely graze and run.
Now arises sentience. It sings
A deeper tone of my complexity.
To the night it turns, fractured,
Lost in the folds of a darker hue...
Until dawns a wiser morning.
Then, awakened, sentience
Remembers its true nature,
And shaking free its earthly shadows,
Rises to meet itself again, singing,
"I have donned my earthly gown
To stray in Self-created dream."

August 2010

You-Me-Us

It isn't just about *me*.
It's also about how I may serve *you*.
How I may interweave
Kindness into all my actions,
Light into all my judgements,
Honesty into all my encounters.
So that you are valued for yourself
And I am myself made better
In both your company and in my own.
Ultimately it isn't about *you* or *me* at all!
It is about *us*
And how each weaves the world
Out of her highest inspiration,
And her purest intention.
We dream
The best of ourselves
Into the world.
And
We are infinitely greater
Than we have so far imagined.

August 2017

In honour of

Margaret Helgason Decosse
My darling, beautiful, and talented
Mother, my sister, my friend,
For all her precious hopes and her dreams
For her courageous, feisty, and loving heart
But mostly for all that she was.

Louise
2021

In honour of

Foch Roland Decosse,
For all the car rides and the sunsets,
My dear father and fierce protector.
My guide of reason and of discernment.
Still with us at over one hundred years old.
He teaches us the elegance
And the dignity of growing old.

Louise
2021

Author's Note

Why are the concepts of "voice" and "callings" so important in this collection of poetry? And why such focus on Jeanne d'Arc's quatrain?

I have always felt a connection with Jeanne and her "voices", based on a powerful experience I had as a child, and on significant dreams and personal explorations which came after. When I first read Jeanne's quatrain, I was moved by its beautiful simplicity and honesty. I recognized how a voice could come out of nowhere in a most unexpected way and in quite ordinary circumstances. At times in my life, I would hear a distinct voice teaching me, guiding me or commenting. I came to recognize that a higher wisdom than my own was at play, often bringing me to a small awakening. This voice became a friendly presence and an inspiration.

Over time, I have come to consider the possibility that there might be another realm, outside time and space, outside all materiality and physicality, to which we might have access, and from which these experiences come. It may be said that in poetry, I found my voice, or that I found the courage to express my own understanding of reality, something that contradicts the much-entrenched dogma of materialism upon which much of our civilization rests.

The Voice

The concept of a "voice" is many-layered and complex and suggests the possibility that a transformation in consciousness is inherent. I quoted Jeanne because I recognized that there is the minor presence of an interior but audible voice scattered throughout my own poetry. I have called the voice my Dream Teacher, my Inner Companion or my Inner Voice.

I find myself unable to deny the experience of having words and messages, some audible and some not, come spilling out of my mind, my mouth, my dreams, out of silence...or just out of the blue. When I was a child, I hardly knew the real origin of the experience, or if, as when I was a young woman, it was merely an aspect of my own subconscious. Understanding so little at the time, I took the experience for granted as the common experience shared by everyone. Today, I am more prepared to state that it is not psychological or "woo-woo", it is of the psyche and of the metaphysical and objectively real. I am aware others are having similar experiences and that the conversation is more open and more widespread than ever before.

The experience appears to describe what the Islamic scholar Henry Corbin called an encounter with the realm of the imaginal, or the *mundus imaginalis*. According to him, the imaginal realm must be understood as real, unrelated to the imagination, to the imaginary, to fantasy, or to make-believe.

Callings

To me, everything is a calling, an attraction, an invitation to pay attention. But attention is not enough on its own. It asks an openness on one's part, and an availability. If *it* is calling you, *it* has something to offer you that is important. But *it* must be understood by you at some level, at least to the degree that your attention has been drawn to *it* and you consent to look or to listen deeply and try to discern something of *its* message. There comes a third part, and that is your willingness to allow *it* some degree of integration within yourself.

At this point you have entered a deeper relationship with the "caller" and, if your state of openness is sufficient, you probably care a fair amount about that caller, or at least you are intrigued enough to investigate *its* message. At best, you desire to invest yourself with the calling. But always there is the freedom to do or not to do so, and up to what point.

At other times it may be that you "fall into the moment" and are fully and gloriously absorbed. The rest is a wonderful experience of encounter or of insight to which you are fully present and aware; in silence, in an *"Aha!" moment*, in an arrested moment.

Who was calling whom? Or did you just bump into each other unexpectedly?

Of course, callings do come in different shades. It is always an individual's responsibility to discern, to filter a calling through the heart, for there are invitations that mislead.

I have also found that callings come with gifts...subtle shifts of mood or attitude, and always for the good. They occur inside oneself...a tiny surge of happiness, unity, delight, understanding, connection, balance, compassion...a new opening of sort. And staying open enough to recognize these tiny callings strengthens, deepens, and sensitizes you in time...in the way you see yourself, the other, the world, in your relationship with these. It shapes you in time, and the life-path you will pursue. *Callings are important.*

The Poetry

I was recently diagnosed with a condition that suddenly caused an onset of excruciating pain. I looked into my husband's eyes and saw the depth of his distress on my behalf. I wrapped my arms around his neck and told him, "This pain is really terrible, *but it's only a layer of my experience*! Under that layer lies the core of me and I'm happy! So, screw the pain! The happiness is so much more enduring and real, and don't you forget it!"

My poems are an expression of that core of happiness. Beneath every pain, misery, and atrocity lies the exquisite flower of one's being, the potential for happiness, despite what life may throw at us. It is my experience and my faith that beauty, goodness, and light are the core of our spiritual reality. They put into question the power we give to all those layers of pain and despair. It seems that, as individuals and as a collective, the path we eventually choose *is* usually our own. Love and beauty are core values, and a choice. Along with them come compassion and a certain purity of being. Ultimately, what makes us stronger and wiser is learning to courageously self-correct along the way, keeping an eye always toward those higher values, while also recognizing our many human failings.

"I am more than my physical body!" declared Robert A. (Bob) Monroe. The potentials are vast and significant to our outcome and to humanity's. I believe that we are creatures endowed with awareness, beauty and brilliance: angels and demons on the one hand, perhaps, until we come to realize who and what we really are. Is there more? That has always been the big question. It is one to which I answer with all my heart: Yes!

I have learned that we cannot save others like some superman or superwoman. We cannot "save" the world in that way. We can only deal with our own self and stand up with others in compassionate fellowship. *We can plant a seed*, be the pebble that makes ripples in the water. These poems are a celebration, a refusal to live life in the darker layers and they are a repetition of the claim: *I know there is more to life.*

There is exquisite beauty in the world. At its core, there is curiosity, goodness, and light. Love is the expression of light. Beauty is a mystery, and I seek it with an inner delight and joy. It inspires and impassions me to write about it, to stand witness to its incredible possibilities of generosity and goodness. We get to choose! Right now!

Perhaps one or several of these poems could be a calling, (*Callings Volume 1)* for someone. As could a spider? Or a song? All these poems are gentle offerings to the universe, offerings which I lightly toss to the wind, perhaps like *Petals (Volume 2)*. To quote one of them:

> *For this is my tenderly planted garden,*
> *Each flower lovingly placed for eternity.*

And *Wording* (Volume 3), is my attempt to recover and weave together the wonderful, intimate, full, and organic green pathways of the language of relationship, to protect it from the threat of an invasive, impersonal, techno-language, which offers only a flatness, and death to the soul of matter.

And finally

This poetry strains everywhere it can to say something about the deep feminine soul. It wants to acknowledge her, to announce her coming to consciousness again. It is a profound cosmic event that is happening, that has been much longed for and awaited. She is The Green Woman; she is Psyche; she is Sophia, and she dwells in the light-live body of the world, of language, and of the heart. She is calling us to her ever more insistently.

I rejoice in the light-live body of the world!

Louise Stefania Decosse

Edmonton, Alberta
April 2021